YOU CHOOSE

CAN YOU SURVIVE the Schoolchildren's BLIZZARD?

AN INTERACTIVE HISTORY ADVENTURE

by Ailynn Collins

CAPSTONE PRESS
a capstone imprint

Published by Capstone Press, an imprint of Capstone.
1710 Roe Crest Drive
North Mankato, Minnesota 56003
capstonepub.com

Copyright © 2022 by Capstone. All rights reserved. No part of this publication may be reproduced in whole or in part, or stored in a retrieval system, or transmitted in any form or by any means, electronic, mechanical, photocopying, recording, or otherwise, without written permission of the publisher.

Library of Congress Cataloging-in-Publication Data
Names: Collins, Ailynn, 1964– author.
Title: Can you survive the schoolchildren's blizzard? : an interactive history adventure / Ailynn Collins.
Description: North Mankato, Minnesota : Capstone Press, an imprint of Capstone, [2022] | Series: You choose: disasters in history | Includes bibliographical references and index. | Audience: Ages 8–12. | Audience: Grades 4–6. | Summary: "It is January 12, 1888, and you are caught by surprise by a powerful blizzard that sweeps across the Midwest. Dangerously cold temperatures, high winds, and deep snow make travel nearly impossible. Will you be able to find your way home through the storm after leaving school? Can you find your father after he becomes lost in the blinding snow? Will you be able to help your students find shelter after the storm ruins your schoolhouse? With dozens of possible choices, it's up to YOU to find a way to survive one of history's worst blizzards"--Provided by publisher.
Identifiers: LCCN 2021033276 (print) | LCCN 2021033277 (ebook) | ISBN 9781663958969 (hardcover) | ISBN 9781666323719 (paperback) | ISBN 9781666323726 (pdf)
Subjects: LCSH: Blizzards--Middle West--History--19th century--Juvenile literature. | Frontier and pioneer life--Middle West--Juvenile literature. | Hypothermia--Middle West--History--19th century--Juvenile literature. | Survival--Juvenile literature. | Middle West--History--19th century--Juvenile literature.
Classification: LCC F595 .C697 2022 (print) | LCC F595 (ebook) | DDC 977/.031--dc23
LC record available at https://lccn.loc.gov/2021033276
LC ebook record available at https://lccn.loc.gov/2021033277

Editorial Credits
Editor: Aaron Sautter; Designer: Bobbie Nuytten; Media Researcher: Morgan Walters; Production Specialist: Laura Manthe

All internet sites appearing in back matter were available and accurate when this book was sent to press.

Printed and bound in China. 5378

TABLE OF CONTENTS

About Your Adventure 5

CHAPTER 1
A New Life 7

CHAPTER 2
A Close Call 11

CHAPTER 3
A Long Walk Home 45

CHAPTER 4
A Teacher's Tale 77

CHAPTER 5
A Deadly Day 103

More About Winter Weather 106
Other Paths to Explore 108
Bibliography 109
Glossary 110
Read More 111
Internet Sites 111
About the Author 112

ABOUT YOUR ADVENTURE

YOU are living in the midwestern United States in the late 1800s. Life is difficult on the plains. The land is tough to farm, and the weather is unpredictable. Summers can be hot and dry, and winters can be brutally cold.

One day in January 1888, you experience one of the worst winter storms anyone has ever seen. Surrounded by snow, howling winds, and plunging temperatures, will YOU survive the storm's fury?

Chapter One sets the scene. Then you choose which path to read. Follow the directions at the bottom of the page as you read the stories. The decisions you make will change your outcome. After you finish one path, go back and read the others for new perspectives and more adventures.

Turn the page to begin your adventure.

The Homestead Act helped almost 4 million people settle on land in the western United States.

CHAPTER 1
A NEW LIFE

On May 20, 1862, U.S. President Abraham Lincoln signed a law called the Homestead Act. If you were at least 21 years old, you could claim 160 acres (65 hectares) of land. Most of the land was west of the Mississippi River. It didn't matter what your background or race was. All you had to do was build a home on the land and farm it for five years. After that, the land was all yours.

This act drew many people to states and territories in the American Midwest such as Minnesota, the Dakota Territory, Nebraska, and Iowa. People came from cities like New York or Boston, hoping that farming would bring them a better life.

Turn the page.

Some people came all the way from countries like Germany, Norway, and Ukraine. Wars and bad rulers made it impossible to live there, and many families were starving. On the other hand, the Midwest had plenty of open, free land for farmers who were willing to work.

But for those who made the journey, life here is hard. The weather is severe, and the pests are dangerous. Farming is unpredictable, and the science of weather forecasting is still new.

The winter of 1887 has been especially cold. From before Christmas to the New Year, families have stayed indoors to stay warm. Schools have remained closed. And when farmers leave the house to feed their animals, they cross quickly to their barns. They do their chores as quickly as possible to return to their warm homes.

Then on January 12, 1888, people wake up to a warm, sunny day. Well, at least it seems warm compared to the recent subzero temperatures. It feels like spring has arrived early.

Unfortunately, this day is about to turn into one of the worst natural disasters in history. A powerful blizzard unlike any people have ever seen is about to hit. Many will be caught in the historic storm, and many will not survive.

To be a young boy from the big city, turn to page 11.

To be an 11-year-old girl on her survival adventure, turn to page 45.

To journey as a young teacher, turn to page 77.

The small town of Yankton became the official capital of the Dakota Territory in 1861.

CHAPTER 2
A CLOSE CALL

Your family arrives in Yankton, Dakota Territory, in the late fall. You're disappointed. It isn't much of a town. It's nothing like your home city of Boston, Massachusetts.

"I miss my old school," your big brother William complains. He didn't want to leave the big city to come out west.

"Think of how much good we can do here," Father says. He's set up his law offices in the middle of town.

"I can't wait to play my tricks on the teacher," you say with a grin.

"Walter, be on your best behavior," Mother warns. "Your last teacher almost quit because of your mischief."

Turn the page.

Still, you can't wait. Unfortunately, winter came early. It's been so harsh that school is canceled until it warms up.

Mr. Cooper, your teacher, rents a room in your family's large house. He insists that you practice writing your letters every day. It's so boring!

"No one else is doing schoolwork," you complain one bright morning. "Especially when the sun is shining like this."

Mr. Cooper looks outside. "You're right," he says. "It feels nice enough to start school."

It's been weeks since it's been this warm. The air feels almost as if spring is on its way.

"I'm going to open up the school today," Mr. Cooper says. "You go pack your bag and meet me at school."

To ignore Mr. Cooper, go to page 13.
To get ready for school, turn to page 18.

Although you're eager to go back to school, you've been cooped up in the house for weeks. The whole time you've been doing homework under Mr. Cooper's watchful eye. You deserve a break.

You decide to sneak into the alley between your house and the neighbor's. You spend the morning building snowmen and a fort instead. You even plan to start a snowball fight with William when he gets back. This time, you'll win. You're sure of it.

But as you're making plans, the alley suddenly goes dark. You look up to see that the sky has gone black. You hear a loud roar just as a strong gust of wind knocks you onto your back.

You smack into the wall of your snow fort. The breath is knocked out of you, and you lie on the ground a little too long. The wind howls, and sharp, painful bits of snow pelt your face. You can barely see in front of you.

Turn the page.

You force yourself up to your feet and desperately feel for the wall that is your house. You take several steps but you can't find your way. You rub your eyes, but the snow on your gloves freezes your eyes shut. Rubbing them just makes it hurt more.

You decide to turn and see if you can find shelter.

To head left, go to page 15.
To go to the right, turn to page 17.

You turn and stumble about with your arms in front of you. It's getting hard to breathe. You want to cry but your tears freeze as they leave your eyes. It hurts.

THUMP! Your hands hit something solid. It's not snow. It's wood!

It must be my house, you say to yourself.

You follow the wall all the way to the front side of the house and the door. You turn the knob and push your way inside. After you slip inside, you slide down to the floor. Then you hear footsteps and voices coming toward you.

Soon you feel someone lift you to your feet. It's Mother. She puts you by the fire and helps to warm you up.

"How did you get stuck outside?" she asks. "I thought you were at school."

Turn the page.

You begin to cry. The tears sting your face. You tell her how you ignored Mr. Cooper's instructions.

"I'm so sorry," you cry.

Mother hugs you tight. "I'm just glad you're inside and safe."

You and Mother ride out the storm in the comfort of your warm home.

THE END

To follow another path, turn to page 9.
To learn more about the blizzard, turn to page 103.

You turn to your right and start walking. You wander about aimlessly for what seems like hours. Still no house.

"Help!" You cry out, but no one can hear you above the wind.

Eventually you bump into the wall of your snow fort again. You slide down next to it, hoping it will shield you from the wind. Exhausted from wandering in the cold and snow, you soon pass out.

Two days later, your brother William finds your body. Instead of playing pranks at school, you're one of the first victims of the historic blizzard.

THE END

To follow another path, turn to page 9.
To learn more about the blizzard, turn to page 103.

As you get ready for school, Mother comes to your room and gives you a crystal glass bottle. It has beautiful patterns in the glass, and it sparkles just like snow.

"You can use this bottle for water to clean your slate at school," Mother says. "Be sure to take care of it."

The bottle is the most precious thing you have. You promise your mother that you'll take the best care of it. You gently place it into your bag, careful to cushion it in a safe corner. As you head downstairs, Mother stops to look out the window.

"Goodness, I'm not sure Walter should go to school today," she says.

"Of course, he should go," Father says, putting on his coat. He and William are ready to leave for the office.

"I have a bad feeling about this strange weather," Mother says.

"But I want to go to school!" you wail.

Mother insists that you stay. But Father says it'll be safe.

To stay at home with Mother, turn to page 20.

To go to school, turn to page 28.

"No, I've already decided," Mother says. "My little Walter will stay home with me today."

You stomp your feet for good measure, but it doesn't make you feel better.

"Don't worry," Mother says comfortingly. "If the weather has truly turned, there'll be school again tomorrow."

You spend the day doodling on your slate and draw silly pictures of Mr. Cooper. It's fun for a while, but soon you feel bored.

Suddenly, it gets dark in your room, but it isn't even lunchtime yet. You look outside and see dark clouds roaring into town. The wind blows so hard that your window flies open. It's a struggle to close it again. You shiver as you lock the window shut.

You stare as the storm clouds turn the day into night. Snow falls heavily, but the small flakes are blowing sideways. They hit your window like tiny pebbles.

"Mother, come and see this," you call as you head into the living room.

During the storm, it was nearly impossible to see through the heavy, windblown snow.

Turn the page.

But she's not there. You search everywhere in the house for her. She's not home. You pick up a candle and light it. The house has never felt so big and so lonely.

"She must have gone to Father's office," you say aloud.

You wait in the living room for what feels like hours. The storm grows louder, and the house turns cold. You're really scared now. Father's office isn't far, just across the street. You're sure that your whole family is enjoying the large fireplace there. They're probably laughing about you being alone in the big house. The anger inside you grows.

To go outside to look for Mother, go to page 23.

To stay in the house, turn to page 26.

You put on your heaviest coat and head to the door. As you open it, the wind pushes you backward. The snow pelts your face like hundreds of tiny bug bites. You wrap your scarf tightly around your face, leaving only your eyes visible.

When you step outside it's so dark you can't even see your hand in front of you. But you know that if you walk straight, you'll get to Father's office on the other side of Main Street.

You take a few steps away from the house. Icicles freeze on your eyelashes. You squeeze your eyelids shut, but the cold freezes them together.

This is too hard. You turn around and head back toward your house. You put your arms out in front of you to feel for the door. But it isn't there—just freezing darkness.

Turn the page.

Your heart leaps into your throat. Where did the house go? You're sure you only took a few steps out of the house. Your mind goes fuzzy. You don't know which way you're facing, and the house is nowhere to be found.

"Help!" You call out, but your voice is carried away by the storm.

You turn again and take a few more steps. Which way is which? You have to keep going. You face the wind and push your way through the storm. You can't feel your hands or feet, and you can't see through your frozen eyelashes.

BAM! You slam into something hard.

"What's this?" You hear a familiar voice. Then you feel arms wrap around you.

"Walter? What are you doing out here?" You recognize Father's voice now.

"Hurry, let's get inside," Mother says. She sounds so far away.

The next thing you know, you're back in your house. William lights the candles, and Father starts a fire. Mother warms you with tea.

"Why would you do something so dangerous?" she asks.

"I was scared to be alone," you sob. But these are tears of happiness.

"You're so small, the wind could've easily carried you away," William teases.

You just smile. You don't care if William treats you like a small child. You only care that your family is all safe at home.

THE END

To follow another path, turn to page 9.
To learn more about the blizzard, turn to page 103.

You decide the smart thing to do is wait for Mother to return. As you wait, boredom takes over and you soon fall asleep.

WHAM!

You wake with a start when the front door slams open. The storm is now roaring inside your house! Did the wind rip the front door off its hinges? But then you hear the sound of boots stomping in the hallway.

"Who's there?" you cry. "Mother? Father? Is that you?"

You wrap yourself in a blanket and stumble to the dark hallway. You hear familiar voices. It's your family! Your father is lighting a few candles as William secures the front door.

"I was so worried about you!" Mother says. "I went out to bring Father and William home."

Settlers stayed safe and warm indoors during severe winter storms.

"It's terrifying out there," William says. He shakes a mound of snow off himself and onto the floor. "It's a good thing you listened to Mother's advice. I can't imagine how the schoolchildren are handling this storm."

As you hug your mother, you're glad you listened to her.

THE END

To follow another path, turn to page 9.
To learn more about the blizzard, turn to page 103.

Mother doesn't like it but won't stop you from going to school. However, she insists you wear your heavy coat, even though it's far too warm for that. Still, you obey just so she'll let you go.

"Glad you made it," says Mr. Cooper as you climb the stairs to his second-story classroom. When you get there, you see that no one else is wearing a thick coat.

"It's too warm!" a girl named Mary says. She didn't even wear her wool stockings to school.

"Who needs a coat on a day like today?" adds a boy named Sam. "It's practically spring!"

You quickly hang up your coat and look for a seat. You carefully place your special water bottle inside your desk and prepare for the day's lessons.

Mr. Cooper grins at you. "Why don't we have our newest student read aloud today?"

You swell with pride. You're a great reader, and you love to show off your skills. But, because you also love pranks, you decide to read in a funny voice.

Soon, the classroom is filled with giggles. Mr. Cooper looks disappointed. You see that he's about to stop you when his eyes turn to the window. His face grows pale.

"What's that roaring sound?" Mary cries.

"I've never seen clouds move so fast!" Sam says. Everyone runs to the window. The sky has gone completely dark.

Mr. Cooper leaves the room to talk with the other teachers. When he returns he gets everyone's attention.

Turn the page.

In the 1800s, children on the plains often attended school in small, one-room buildings.

"Children, we're sending you home—immediately."

But outside the snow has already begun to fall. Within minutes, it's turned into a blinding blizzard. The wind roars like a train rumbling past the school.

Mr. Cooper orders the older children to lock the windows tight. It takes several tries because the wind keeps blowing them open. It gets very cold in the classroom.

"Sit closer to the fire," Mr. Cooper says. Everyone huddles around the stove in the middle of the room, but you're still cold.

CRRRRNCH! BANG!

Mr. Cooper checks the corridor. "The storm's ripping through the roof!"

He bolts the door to your classroom shut to keep out the cold. The younger children begin to cry. You shiver.

The banging grows louder. Has the storm pulled off the entire roof?

To huddle closer to the other students, turn to page 32.

To call out for help, turn to page 33.

RRRIIPP!

It's the loudest sound you've ever heard. The entire building shakes through the floor and into your bones. You can barely catch your breath as icy snow falls through the ripped-open roof.

The cold and wind is too much for your stove. You huddle closer to your classmates, but nothing brings you warmth.

When the storm blows over, the town finds the entire second floor of the schoolhouse has been destroyed. The upper rooms hold the children who didn't make it.

"If only they had moved to the lower rooms," the mayor of the town says later on, "they might have all survived."

THE END

To follow another path, turn to page 9.
To learn more about the blizzard, turn to page 103.

"Help! Someone help us!" you scream.

BANG! BANG! BANG!

"Someone is knocking," says Mr. Cooper. He opens the door to find Mary's father there.

"We're here to take the children home," he tells the teachers. "But we'd better hurry. We can barely see anything already."

Everyone rushes downstairs. You're last to leave the room. By the time you step outside, you can just make out several drays waiting. You've seen these carts in town carrying bags of supplies for farmers. Now they're full of children. The last dray has just enough space for you. As you step outside, the snow feels like sand pelting your face.

"All students are accounted for," shouts Mr. Cooper. The horses pull away, and you're jerked about. It's so cold and dark . . . you can't wait to get home where it's warm and safe.

Turn the page.

During the late 1800s, people often traveled on horse-drawn sleds called drays in winter.

But wait! You forgot the bottle! You left it in your desk. If you don't get it, the water inside will freeze and burst the glass. Mother will be so angry if it's destroyed.

The dray is moving very slowly. You're sure that if you run and get the bottle, the dray won't be too far away when you come back.

To jump off and get the bottle, go to page 35.
To leave the bottle behind, turn to page 41.

It only takes a few seconds to run back and get your bottle. But when you get back outside, you can't see or hear the drays or the horses. There's nothing but the storm.

The snow clogs up your nostrils. Your eyelashes are frozen. Ice flies into your coat and you feel like a frozen icicle. You try to scream, but you hear nothing except the wind. No one is coming for you.

The schoolhouse door creaks as it's about to be blown shut. You catch it just before it locks you out. You could go back inside and hope someone comes looking for you. Or should you try to walk home in this blizzard?

> To go back into the school, turn to page 36.
> To try to get home, turn to page 38.

Just before the door slams shut, you squeeze back inside the schoolhouse. It's eerie and dark—and freezing. You head back upstairs to your classroom, but the roof is gone! Instead, you run back and lock yourself in one of the ground floor classrooms. The wind outside roars loudly. Will the storm tear the building in half—with you inside?

The classroom stove is still warm, but the fire is dying. You find a few pieces of coal left in the supply closet and add them to the stove. The warmth makes you feel better. As you sit by the fire, you pick up a book from a nearby desk. You don't feel so alone as you read.

When you run out of coal, you look around for something to burn. Sadly, you end up sacrificing some books. But they don't burn for long. You decide to smash up a chair to burn the wood.

Just as you're about to smash a second chair, the door flies open. There stand your father and brother!

"Let's get out of here," Father yells, as you run into his arms.

Outside the schoolhouse, there's a dray waiting for you.

"You're lucky that Father made them come back for you," William shouts. "These men have risked their lives for you twice now."

You feel ashamed for being so impulsive but relieved that you're safe. You clutch the bottle to your chest. Mother will be glad it's still in one piece.

THE END

To follow another path, turn to page 9.
To learn more about the blizzard, turn to page 103.

Suddenly, the schoolhouse door slams shut behind you. There's no choice now. You'll have to try to get home on your own.

You move as fast as you can. Your house isn't too far away. The blinding snow hurts and your eyes water. Your tears mix with snow and turn your eyelids into icicles. You walk on blindly, unsure if you're headed in the right direction.

A strong gust of wind blows you over onto the road. Your feet feel so heavy that you can't get back up again. Down here on the ground, the snow feels softer. You can't feel the wind either. Before long, you pass out from the cold.

The next thing you know, you feel yourself floating. You hear voices but you can't make out the words. Your body doesn't feel like your own. You fall unconscious again.

When you awaken, you're back home in bed. Your mother is rubbing snow onto your skin!

"It's a miracle he has no frostbite," Mr. Cooper says, worried.

"You'll be fine, Walter," Mother speaks quietly. "You mustn't be warmed up too quickly or your heart will fail. The snow will slow down the warming."

"The snow doesn't feel cold," you say, and it's true. You begin to feel a burning sensation in your hands and feet. It's painful, but at least they're not numb. "How did you find me?"

"Your brother carried you home," Mother says, wiping a tear from her eye.

"I mostly dragged you," William says, appearing at your side.

Turn the page.

"Your brother went back to the school, but you weren't there," Father says. "On the way back, he got on his hands and knees and followed the wagon tracks until he found you. Genius!"

"Or dumb luck," William says. "It was a miracle I found you."

Just then you feel a trickle of cold liquid at your side. You stick a hand into your pocket and pull out a piece of glass.

"Oh no! The bottle broke!" You start to cry.

Your mother kisses you on the head. "It's just a bottle," she says. "You're more precious than anything we own."

You go back to sleep, glad to be safe at home with your family again.

THE END

To follow another path, turn to page 9.
To learn more about the blizzard, turn to page 103.

You want to jump off the dray and run back for the bottle. But when you stand up, the dray suddenly jerks forward. Mr. Cooper grabs your legs to keep you from falling off.

"What are you doing, Walter?" Mr. Cooper scolds.

You don't say anything. Your bottle is doomed. You pull your coat up around you, glad for the bit of protection it gives. You huddle close to Sam and Mary.

The drays haven't gone far, but it's so dark that you can't see the schoolhouse anymore. You realize that if you'd gone back for the bottle, you might have been stuck in the storm.

The dray jerks hard again and comes to a stop.

"The horses can't go any farther," you hear the driver shout. He jumps off and unties the horses. They hobble off into the distance.

Turn the page.

"What do we do now?" Mr. Cooper asks.

The driver, Sam's father, says, "Let's turn the dray upside down and take shelter beneath it."

You work together to do as he says. You can barely feel your hands and feet as you work. You all huddle together for warmth under the dray.

The younger children sob as the wind howls. You try to be brave, but tears fill your eyes. You've never been this scared before. You don't even have your mother's bottle to comfort you.

Just as your body goes completely numb, you hear voices. Several men have come to help. One of them is your father!

The men lift the dray, and you feel someone carry you away. You can't be sure if it's your father. But as soon as you're laid in bed, you know you're home.

"This will help you warm up slowly and safely," Mother explains, rubbing snow into your arms and feet. "If you warm up too quickly, you could lose your limbs."

You don't question her. You're just glad to be out of the blizzard. When you're able to speak again, you apologize for losing her perfume bottle.

Your mother kisses you on the head. "It's just a bottle," she says. "You're more valuable to us than any bottle."

You go back to sleep, happy to be safe at home with your family again.

THE END

To follow another path, turn to page 9.
To learn more about the blizzard, turn to page 103.

There were few trees on the plains to use for wood. Farming families often built small homes from blocks of sod cut from the thick prairie grass.

CHAPTER 3
A LONG WALK HOME

When your parents die of a disease called smallpox, you're sent to live with your Uncle Wilhelm and Aunt Catherina on their farm near Seward, Nebraska. They treat you well, and speak German, just like you do. You help with chores and with looking after your baby cousins.

One day, Uncle Wilhelm is getting ready to go out in the fields. It's been a cold winter, but you've gotten used to following him to tend to the cows.

"Lena, you're 11 now," he says, sliding on his big boots. "It's time you started school."

Turn the page.

The idea of school terrifies you. "They don't speak German there," you say. You've heard neighbors say that the teacher won't let the children speak anything but English. And your English isn't very good.

"You need to mix with others your age," Aunty Catherina says. "And school could help you improve your English."

You beg them to let you stay home and take care of the twins, but they won't hear of it.

"It's for your own good, Lena," says Aunty.

> To disobey your uncle and aunt and hide in the barn, go to page 47.
> To go to school, turn to page 64.

It's a beautiful, sunny day. The temperature is just under freezing. But the winter has been so cold that today feels like a spring day. You told your uncle you'd go to school. But you have another plan.

Aunty gives you a pail with your lunch inside. "Don't lose this pail. It's the only one we have to spare." She waves goodbye as Uncle walks you to the barn.

"First, go over the hill behind the barn and then through the ravine. The school is on the edge of the plowed field on the other side." He makes you repeat it back to him twice so you won't get lost. Then he heads off to the farm to work.

As soon as he's gone, you sneak back into the barn. It's empty except for a few chickens pecking at the floor. You snuggle up in a pile of hay and watch the chickens.

Turn the page.

This is so much better than going to school. You twist some hay together into a doll. You chase the chickens, and you take a long nap. Later in the day, about when you think school should be finished, you hear something.

BOOM! CRRNCH!

You've never heard such a loud sound. You peek outside, and the sky has gone dark. Snow is falling hard. Some of it blows sideways right into your face.

It takes all your strength to push the barn door shut. But then something suddenly pushes it wide open again. Uncle Wilhelm is standing at the door. His beard and eyebrows are white with snow. You're in trouble.

"What are you doing here?" he roars.

You begin to cry.

"No tears," he says quickly. "Help me bring the cows in."

You breathe a sigh of relief. The storm may have just saved you from big trouble.

You wrap yourself in your overcoat and step through the barn door. It's incredibly dark outside. Uncle walks out ahead of you and quickly disappears from sight.

You trudge along, trusting that he's in front of you. The snow blows straight into your face, and your body feels numb. It's hard to breathe. You're about to turn around and head back when you hear the low mooing of the cows. You reach out and bump right into Uncle.

"Get these cows back to the barn!" he shouts.

Turn the page.

A blinding blizzard can be dangerous for both people and animals that are caught in the storm.

You lead the cows back. But when you reach the barn, snow is piled up high against the door. You and Uncle work to remove the snow, but there's too much.

"Why don't we go to the other side?" you suggest. "It might be sheltered from the wind."

"Good idea," Uncle says.

You lead the cows to the other side of the barn. Once they're all inside, you fall into a pile of hay, breathless.

Uncle Wilhelm pats off the mound of snow from his coat. "We should get back to your aunt. She'll be worried."

"Come along, the house is this way," he says, pointing.

"No, sir, it's the other way," you say. "We're on the other side of the barn."

"If that's what you think, then we go our separate ways."

This behavior is strange for your uncle. Maybe the cold has him confused.

To follow your uncle, turn to page 52.
To go the other direction, turn to page 59.

You hold on to Uncle Wilhelm's coat and follow him into the blizzard. His huge body shields you from being pelted by the ice. You put your head down and keep moving.

"Where are the saplings?" he shouts. "Can you see them?"

There's a row of young trees along a path to the house. You should've reached the first one by now. But you don't see anything through the snow. You stretch out with one hand and try to feel your way to the saplings.

Nothing.

"Maybe we haven't gone far enough. We need to find it soon," Uncle shouts. "I can't feel my feet." He takes a step and stumbles onto his knees.

You scream. You're too small to pick up Uncle, and without him, you're sure you'll never find the house. You pull him up by the arm, but he doesn't budge.

"Please, get up!" you cry. "We're almost home."

But your uncle collapses to the ground. He doesn't move or speak.

To stay with Uncle, turn to page 54.
To go for help, turn to page 55.

Your tears freeze into ice on your face. Panic rises inside you. You try to lift your uncle, but he's much too heavy.

You kneel down beside him and bury your face in his warm coat. Maybe if you stay together, you can keep each other warm. Someone is sure to come by and find you.

You huddle in closer and soon fall asleep. It's strange, but the snow feels warmer here on the ground. How can that be?

The next day a neighbor finds both of you, huddled together and frozen. Your aunt is heartbroken. She'll never forget how this cruel storm stole these two precious lives from her.

THE END

To follow another path, turn to page 9.
To learn more about the blizzard, turn to page 103.

"Uncle, please get up!" You try to lift him, but he's a dead weight. Plus, your own arms feel numb from the cold.

"I must get help," you say to yourself. "If I go back the way we came, I'll reach the barn. Then I can try again."

You force yourself up onto your feet. Looking around, you turn your back to the wind and head straight. You can't feel your hands or feet, your eyes burn, and it's hard to breathe. You begin to doubt yourself.

Which way are you headed? It feels like you've been walking for hours. You want to turn back when you run into something hard. You reach out and feel something like the side of a building. Are you back at the barn?

Turn the page.

> Whiteout conditions in a blizzard can cause people to get lost in dangerous freezing weather.

You guide yourself around the building until you find a door. You must be home!

"Help me, Aunty!" You pound the door with your fists.

The door swings open, and you fall inside. It's warm in here, and something smells delicious. But this isn't home.

Your eyes are still frozen shut, but you can hear voices. Someone lifts you off the floor and places you on a soft bed. Then you feel someone remove your boots and scrub your hands and feet with something rough. It doesn't hurt because you can't really feel anything.

After a while, you can move your fingers and toes and open your eyes. At first, everything is a blur. But then you see the kind face of a woman you don't know.

"Hello, dear. I'm Helen," the woman says. A large man appears behind her. "This is my husband, John."

You burst into tears. In your broken English, you try to explain that your uncle's out there in the snow. Mr. John grabs his coat and hat and rushes out to find your uncle. After he leaves, you fall into a deep sleep.

Turn the page.

When you wake, John and Uncle are sitting by the fire, sipping soup from a bowl. The smell makes you hungry. Helen helps you sit up and serves you a bowl of the delicious hot soup.

"I must get home to my wife," Uncle says. "She will worry."

"It's best to stay until the storm is over," John insists.

You spend the night in this cozy home. The next morning, the sun shines again.

The blizzard is over. You're so thankful for your neighbors. For many years to come, you will remain close to Mrs. Helen and Mr. John.

THE END

To follow another path, turn to page 9.
To learn more about the blizzard, turn to page 103.

Uncle Wilhelm leaves you to yourself. You lose sight of him in seconds, and the fierce wind quickly sweeps away his footprints.

The other barn door is blocked by snow. You'll have to go around the barn and try to reach the row of saplings on the other side. Then you can follow them to the house.

You pull your coat tighter around yourself and take a deep breath. The snow hits your face like a million tiny slaps. Your eyelashes freeze almost immediately. It's hard to breathe as your nose fills up with snow. Your lips can barely move.

You feel along the side of the barn until you reach the front. The door's practically hidden by the mountain of snow, but you can just see the lantern that hangs above it. You press your back into the sturdy side of the barn. The house is a hundred steps from this corner, straight ahead.

Turn the page.

With every step forward, the wind seems to blow you two steps to the left. You work hard to correct it, but you soon grow tired. Did you correct the last few steps? You don't remember.

Your eyes burn from the snow and ice. Maybe your uncle was right. You should've stuck together. It feels like you've walked for miles when you collapse to the ground.

Strangely, it feels warmer on the ground. The wind blows just above you, barely touching your back. The snow is softer here. You can't help yourself. You're so tired that you fall asleep.

The next thing you know you're opening your eyes to sunshine. By some miracle, you've made it through the storm!

> To get up and get help, go to page 61.
> To wait to be rescued, turn to page 62.

Slowly, you get up on your feet. But you can't feel your body. Everything is so strange. In the distance, you see two men walking. You wave and try to speak, but your voice doesn't work.

You take a few steps. You feel lighter than usual. The men see you and come running.

"Don't walk," they call. "We're coming to you!"

What an odd thing to say! you think.

Then, without warning, your legs give way. It's hard to catch your breath, and you black out.

Your body has spent all night trying to keep you warm. When you stood up, your heart had to work too hard to pump blood to your arms and legs. Your heart stopped just as the men reached you.

You are another victim of the storm's fury.

THE END

To follow another path, turn to page 9.
To learn more about the blizzard, turn to page 103.

As you blink your eyes in the sunshine, you hear a voice in the distance.

"Lena!" Uncle cries. "You're still alive!"

You push yourself to stand up. It's strange because you can't really feel your body. But suddenly you're standing and waving at Uncle Wilhelm. He looks fine, so you must be too.

Uncle lifts you into his arms just as you feel yourself collapse.

"I turned back to find you and you were gone. I was so worried," he says. "I don't know why I left you in the first place."

You try to speak, but you don't have the energy to say a word.

Uncle Wilhelm talks as he continues toward home. When you reach the house, Aunty gets you out of your wet clothes. She rubs you with snow. It feels warm and strange.

But as they talk of their relief, you pass out. Sadly, you never wake up again. The extreme cold was too much for your heart.

Uncle Wilhelm and Aunty Catherina hold a small funeral for you. You only lived for 11 years. But they'll never forget you.

THE END

To follow another path, turn to page 9.
To learn more about the blizzard, turn to page 103.

You reluctantly agree to go to school. Following Uncle Wilhelm's instructions, you pass by the barn, go up the hill, and down into the ravine. The knot in your stomach tightens with each step.

An hour later, you arrive at the one-room schoolhouse.

"Good morning," the teacher, Miss Badger, says. "You must be Lena." You nod in reply. You don't speak English well, unlike the other kids here.

There are 15 children here of all ages. You spend the day pretending to read the textbook. When no one is looking, you watch the others play and work. At the end of the day, you're the first one ready to go home. Miss Badger stands at the door looking very worried. Outside, dark clouds have rolled in, and snow is falling hard.

She shoos you all back into the classroom. "It's too dangerous to send you home in this blizzard. I can barely see a foot in front of me."

You huddle by the stove with the others to keep warm, but it barely gives off enough heat. You shiver, even as you sit in your coat.

Miss Badger stands up suddenly. "Children, we must go somewhere warmer. My house is near here. We can go there."

The children all line up near the door. When Miss Badger opens it, the wind blows a pile of snow into the schoolroom. In the doorway, there's a man covered in snow.

It's the father of one of the children. "I've brought my wagon to take the children home."

"Thank you," Miss Badger says. "Most of the children live south of here. Only two live to the north."

Turn the page.

Miss Badger and the man look at you. You and the oldest boy, Joshua, both live north of the school.

"The wind is coming from the north," the man says. "It would mean heading into the storm. That's much harder than moving south."

"You two should stay with me," Miss Badger suggests. "Your parents can come for you after the storm blows over."

"Or I can walk home with you," Joshua says. "My house isn't far from yours."

>To go with Miss Badger, go to page 67.
>To walk home with Joshua, turn to page 74.

"Your safety is my responsibility," Miss Badger says. "I insist that you come home with me."

Everyone climbs into the wagon. The snow is blowing sideways, and it fills your nose and mouth. You've never felt this cold in your life.

After a long time, the wagon stops at the first house. One by one, the children are dropped off. Then it's Miss Badger's turn to get off. She takes you by the hand and waves for Joshua to follow.

Once off the wagon, Miss Badger holds your hand tightly. "My house is this way," she says, pointing.

"No, ma'am," says Joshua, pointing in another direction. "I think we need to go this way."

To go with Miss Badger, turn to page 68.
To follow Joshua's advice, turn to page 71.

Through the darkness, you spot the weak yellow light of a lantern.

"That's my front door!" Miss Badger cries. "Thank heavens the lantern is still burning."

She pulls you along to the doorstep. But you can't get to the front door. Too much snow has piled up in front of it. You and Joshua start scooping away the snow, but it's hopeless. You soon can't feel your hands and feet, and the snow piles up as fast as you can scoop it away.

"Maybe we should climb in through a window," Joshua finally offers.

Miss Badger helps him look for an unlocked window. You're the smallest, so they lift you through the window first. Miss Badger follows, and Joshua is last. You're all safe inside.

Miss Badger gives you dry, warm clothes, and you help to light a fire. Joshua puts on a pot to make soup. You're glad to be out of the storm, but it's uncomfortable being in your teacher's house. She and Joshua speak so fast, you barely understand them.

Turn the page.

After finishing your soup, you fall asleep on a cot in the corner of Miss Badger's room. When you finally wake up, your uncle is waiting for you outside. You slept so long that the storm has passed and it's the next day.

All the way home, Uncle tells you how worried he was.

"Maybe it's better you don't go to school until the spring," he says.

You don't say anything, but perhaps the blizzard was a blessing in disguise.

THE END

To follow another path, turn to page 9.
To learn more about the blizzard, turn to page 103.

"I don't think that's right," Miss Badger says doubtfully as the wagon pulls away. "But we can try going that way first."

You push through the snow for a while, but don't find a building. "Where's the house?" you ask, but the wind is too loud. No one can hear you.

Soon you think you see the yellow glow of a lantern ahead. You tug at her hand and point in the direction of the lantern.

"Stop fooling around," Miss Badger scolds. "Follow me."

That's when you both realize that Joshua is nowhere to be seen. Together you call for the boy. There's no answer.

Miss Badger squeezes your hand. "I'm turned around!" she cries. "Which way is the house?"

You pull her hand again and point in the direction of the light.

Turn the page.

Miss Badger sighs and heads in the direction you were pointing. You both trudge slowly, pushing against the freezing wind.

Suddenly you trip over something and land flat on your face. Miss Badger screams. She grabs you by the back of your coat and practically lifts you back up on your feet.

"Joshua!" you cry, looking down. You've tripped over his body.

Together, you and Miss Badger lift up the boy. He's out cold and is very heavy.

You stumble along, dragging Joshua between you, until you reach the front porch of the house. Miss Badger bangs on the front door. An older lady opens the door to let you in.

"This is my aunt," Miss Badger says. "I live with her."

"Don't sit too near," her aunt says as you approach the fire. "You cannot warm up too quickly." She helps you change into some warm, dry clothes.

Soon Joshua wakes up and joins you near the fire. Miss Badger gives you both a cup of hot tea, and you sip it slowly. After a time, the storm outside grows quiet. A few hours later, Uncle Wilhelm turns up at the house.

"Thank you for keeping my niece safe," your uncle tells the teacher. "You were very brave."

Miss Badger smiles. "I hope that we'll see Lena at school again when the weather is better. I'm quite sure she saved us all."

Maybe school won't be so bad after all.

THE END

To follow another path, turn to page 9.
To learn more about the blizzard, turn to page 103.

You think you can make it home with Joshua. After the wagon has pulled away, you both walk straight into the storm. The snow is like icy flour. It fills up your nose and mouth, making it hard to breathe. It hurts to keep moving but you must.

"Wrong way!" you shout at Joshua.

"We have to go the long way!" he screams over the wind, pointing at the road ahead. "The ravine is covered in snow. If we fall in, we won't get out."

You refuse to move. You want to go home the way you came to school. When you won't budge, Joshua shouts, "Suit yourself! You go your way, and I'll go mine."

In seconds, Joshua disappears into the darkness. You're all alone. Your body is numb, and your feet feel like blocks of ice. As you walk, you feel the ground sloping downward. You're know you're at the ravine.

But the snow has frozen your eyelashes, and you can barely see. You move ahead into the ravine, but you have a bad feeling that you've wandered off the path. You decide to turn around and go back to the schoolhouse. It shouldn't be far, but you keep walking, and nothing appears in front of you.

Finally, exhausted and blinded by the snow, you collapse in the rut of a field. The last thing you remember is pulling your coat over your head.

By 6:00 p.m. that evening, the darkness is complete. No one knows how many children are stuck out in the snow. Some children survive, but neither you nor Joshua are so lucky. The next day, your body is found by a farmer, only a few yards from the schoolhouse door.

THE END

To follow another path, turn to page 9.
To learn more about the blizzard, turn to page 103.

Teachers in the 1800s often rang a bell to let students know it was time to begin the day's lessons.

CHAPTER 4
A TEACHER'S TALE

You've always wanted to be a teacher. Now at the age of 19, you're teaching at the local school in a farming community in Nebraska. You live with Mr. and Mrs. Hunt in their farmhouse. Your family lives more than 170 miles (274 kilometers) away in a town called Seward.

Your schoolhouse is a one-room sod building. Life as a teacher isn't easy. When the school year began in the fall of 1887, you were full of hope. But by Christmas break you're feeling disheartened. There are fewer than 20 school-age children in the area, and they're often needed on their family farms. On a regular school day, you're lucky if three to five of them show up.

To make things worse, this winter has been particularly cold. School's been closed, and you're

Turn the page.

stuck in the Hunts' house with little to do. Mrs. Hunt tries to cheer you up, but you miss your family.

You spend the days thinking about leaving your job. Surely there's a better job somewhere closer to your family.

To quit teaching and head home, go to page 79.

To keep your job, turn to page 88.

"What a lovely day!" exclaims Mrs. Hunt, one sunny January morning.

But you can only think of one thing. You're going home to your family. You pack your things, ignoring Mrs. Hunt's pleas. It feels like you failed at your job.

"Please tell everyone that school will be closed until a new teacher is found," you tell her.

As you step outside, you notice dark, heavy-looking clouds in the distance. They seem to be coming your way, so you pick up your pace.

RUMBLE!

Just as you're leaving the Hunts' large property, you're hit with a blast of cold air. You look up to see the dark clouds moving faster than any you've ever seen. Within moments, the whole area is plunged into night, even though it's barely even lunch time.

Turn the page.

Snow blows sideways in sheets of sharp pellets that bite at your face. The wind is so strong that you can barely stand up straight.

You've only just passed the Hunts' fence. *Surely, I can follow it back to the house,* you think. You turn back and pray for guidance. Within a few minutes, you run into the fence.

You hang on tightly to the fence, even as the wind tries to blow you away. You walk along the fence for what feels like hours. You're numb and confused about where you're going.

Maybe I'm at the wrong fence, you think. You pray aloud, asking for divine help.

"Etta! Etta! Where are you?" Someone's calling your name. It sounds like your father. But your family isn't here. Who could be calling you?

To head toward the voice, go to page 81.
To keep going along the fence, turn to page 84.

"Etta! Follow my voice!"

You realize that the voice belongs to Mr. Hunt. You let go of the fence and walk in the direction of his voice.

As you walk, the wind keeps pushing you. You try to head in the right direction, but it isn't easy. In the distance you see the yellow flicker of lamp light.

"I am saved!" you exclaim.

Farmers in the early United States often built rugged wooden fences to mark the edge of their property and to keep animals from wandering away.

Turn the page.

The snow and cold seeps through your coat as you plow forward. You can't feel your fingers or toes. As you take another step, you stumble to your hands and knees. The rough ground cuts into your skin, but you feel no pain. As you tuck your hands around your waist, you feel something warm and red seeping through your clothes. It freezes within seconds. Your hands are bleeding.

"Dear God, please save me!" you cry.

You want nothing more than to lie down on the ground and rest. Maybe when you've regained some strength, you could find your way to the house again.

You begin to collapse, but you never reach the ground. Large arms catch you and lift you up. Within moments, you're lying on something soft. You feel someone rub your arms and legs with something rough. You can't tell if it's cold or hot.

"Goodness, miss," says a familiar voice. "We almost lost you there."

It's Mrs. Hunt. She's trying to warm you back up. You begin to cry and surprisingly, the ice around your eyes melts. You open your eyes again and see the lovely sight of your hostess taking care of you.

You're so grateful to your hosts. Without them you surely would have perished in this storm.

A week later, you're on your way back to your family in Seward. You're glad you left your job. Being with family is more important to you. You find another job near home and continue teaching for the rest of your life. You stay in touch with the Hunts for many years.

THE END

To follow another path, turn to page 9.
To learn more about the blizzard, turn to page 103.

The voices you're hearing must be in your head. You decide to keep following the fence. But soon your fingers are too numb to feel the wooden posts.

You trip over something and find yourself on your hands and knees. Strangely, it feels warmer here on the ground. It's as if the snow is blowing over you.

You decide to stay down and crawl under the fence. You're sure you're in the pasture. If you keep going, you should end up at the farmhouse.

You sing a favorite hymn as you go. You believe, as you always have, that God has a purpose for you. You're not meant to die here. So with hope in your heart, you keep crawling.

"Please help me find shelter," you pray.

Suddenly, like a miracle, a haystack appears in front of you. You dig your way into the hay and cover yourself with it.

The hay gradually hardens around you, but you don't care. You fall asleep, utterly exhausted. The last thing you remember is praying for the strength to get up again.

When you wake up, it seems to be lighter outside.

A farmer is sure to find me eventually, you think.

You notice something nibbling at your wrists. Mice have found refuge in the haystack too. It comforts you that other creatures have survived this storm. You try to move, but the hay is so frozen that you can't. You lie there and wait. Eventually you drift off to sleep again.

You're dreaming of sitting by a warm fire with your family when you awaken. You're back in the Hunts' home.

"It's a miracle," says a familiar voice. You turn to see your parents by your side.

Turn the page.

"How are you here?" you ask weakly.

"My dear," your mother says, weeping. "You were missing for 78 hours. It's a miracle you survived so long without warmth, food, or water."

"We came as soon as we heard," your father adds. "God has saved you, my child."

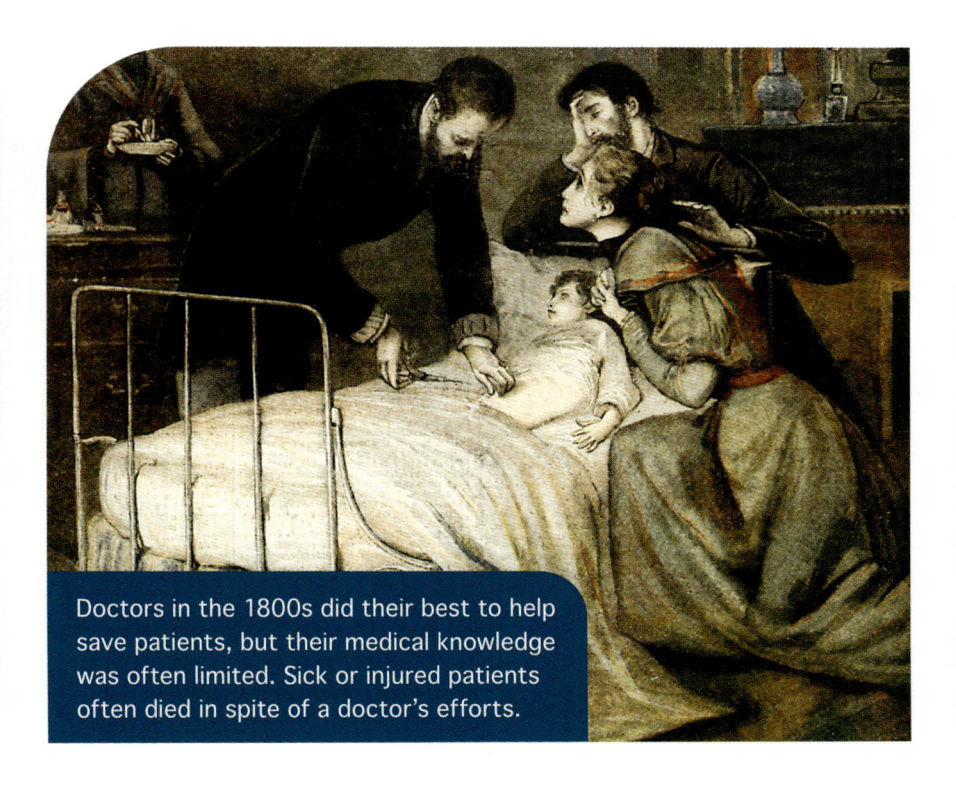

Doctors in the 1800s did their best to help save patients, but their medical knowledge was often limited. Sick or injured patients often died in spite of a doctor's efforts.

You stay in bed for several days. You have severe frostbite. The only way to save your life is to amputate your legs.

The procedure is expensive. However, news of your miraculous survival has reached the newspapers in the surrounding towns. People donate money to help cover the medical expenses. Many people are rooting for you to recover.

Thankfully, the surgery goes well. But three weeks later, you catch pneumonia, and you develop a terrible infection called sepsis.

Early one morning, you die peacefully, surrounded by your family. Many people mourn your death.

THE END

To follow another path, turn to page 9.
To learn more about the blizzard, turn to page 103.

Schools should've already restarted in early January 1888. But the winter has been too harsh to open them. The safety of the children must come first. But when you wake up on January 12, the sky is sunny and bright blue. When you walk outside it feels as if winter is over. Spring has come early this year.

Before the blizzard arrived, the day started out warm and sunny. Many people didn't even wear coats because of the pleasant springlike weather.

"You should open up the school," Mrs. Hunt says. "It'll be good for both you and the children who've been cooped up all winter."

That's a great idea. You head out to spread the word that the school will be open today. Many people are already outside having fun in the sun.

Later, 12 students show up to school. They're happy to see you after being stuck at home for so long. It's so warm that most of them came to school without a heavy coat. You happily begin teaching lessons. This is one of the best mornings you've had in a long time.

But just before noon, the sky changes color. A thundering roar brings clouds racing in overhead. The tiny schoolhouse is plunged into darkness. The wind is so strong that it rattles the roof. The temperature drops quickly.

Turn the page.

You gather the children around the small stove in the middle of the room. There isn't much fuel to burn. It's hard to talk because the storm is so loud outside. You gather all the coats you can find and wrap them around your students. But they're still cold.

WHAM!

Suddenly, a strong blast of wind tears the front door off its hinges. The children scream as snow pours into the classroom. It's hard for you to keep them huddled together. You must act, fast!

To try to fix the school's door, go to page 91.

To try to take the children to your home, turn to page 93.

With the help of the two oldest boys, you bolt the door shut. Thankfully, it keeps the snow out. But the wind also threatens to damage the roof. You have no way to fix that if it's blown off.

It's still freezing in the room. You need fuel. As much as you hate the idea, you decide to burn some textbooks. Then you break a few of the slates that the children write on and burn those.

"Let's break apart a bench," you suggest.

The bigger children help by stomping on a large bench. The oldest boy, John, slams it on the ground several times until it finally breaks.

You burn the wood from the bench, and it provides some warmth. But the children won't stop crying. You wonder why no one has arrived to help. From the sound of the storm outside, it must be so bad that no one can get to you.

Turn the page.

The storm's fierce winds and heavy snow wrecked the roofs of many buildings.

When the storm suddenly rips a corner off the schoolhouse roof, you know you have no choice. Your house isn't far from the school. You must get the children to safety.

Your house isn't far. Your students will be safer there. You rip off a section of your skirt and use the fabric to make a rope. You tie it around each child's wrist.

"We must stick together!" you shout over the loud wind. "Hold on tight to the rope. We don't want to lose anyone."

You're in the front of the line, and John takes up the rear. Outside, the snow hits you right in the face. It feels like frozen sand is filling your nose and mouth. Your eyes burn, and you can barely see anything in front of you. But you have a good sense of direction. You know your house is just over the small hill, right in front of you.

Slowly, you trudge against the wind and snow. You can feel the tug on the fabric rope as the children follow you. You feel the ground beneath you rise as you get closer to home.

Turn the page.

Suddenly, the rope pulls you back. One of the smaller children, Addie, has stumbled. You pick her up and carry her. She feels stiff and frozen like an icicle.

"We're almost there," you say.

The journey goes slowly. With each step you feel the tug of the rope, and the child in your arms feels heavier.

"Please, God, save us!" you pray aloud.

Suddenly, a haystack looms in front of you.

To take shelter in the haystack, go to page 95.

To keep searching for your farmhouse, turn to page 100.

Luckily, the older boys find pitchforks and dig a hole in the frozen haystack large enough for all the children. You huddle together and pray that someone will come and save you.

"Let's shout for help," you suggest. "Together we can be louder than the wind!"

You all shout, but the wind drowns you out. To stop the children from crying, you decide to try a roll call.

Some people took shelter in haystacks they found while wandering in the blizzard.

Turn the page.

"John..."

"Present."

"Fred..."

"Present."

"Addie..."

Addie's fallen asleep. You try to keep the others awake. But soon each child falls asleep. Eventually, you drift off as well. When you wake, the storm is over. You try to move, but you can't feel your arms or legs.

"Children, please, wake up," you cry, but no one stirs.

Suddenly, John stands up. "I'll go get help," he says.

You watch him walk out into the field. But then he stops and turns back to look at you. Suddenly, he collapses to the ground.

You try desperately to get up. You have to help him. But your legs won't budge. You can only pray for help to come.

Finally, you hear wagon wheels. You raise an arm and hope that the person sees you. Voices shout in the sunlight, and you feel arms lift you out of the hay. Out of the corner of your eye, you watch the men carry out each child.

"John?" you ask.

"Sorry, miss," the man says. "He's gone."

* * *

Later at your house, the Hunts look after you until the doctor arrives.

"Your feet are too frostbitten," he says. "I'll have to amputate them."

You're in shock, but Mrs. Hunt reminds you that you're lucky to be alive.

Turn the page.

"How are the children?" you ask.

"They're recovering," the doctor says. "Little Addie has lost her feet as well. Frostbite is terrible."

"What happened to John?" you ask. "He was walking. He seemed fine."

"Sadly, his heart gave out," the doctor says.

Tears run down your face. John was your student. You should've taken better care of him.

After this terrible event, you move back to be with your family in Seward. Eventually, newspapers report about what they call the Schoolchildren's Blizzard. They say many children died that day. They praise the teachers who saved their students.

Someone discovers that you saved the lives of several students. Your story is printed in the newspapers, and you become quite famous. Someone even composes a song about your heroic efforts to save the children.

But you don't feel like a hero. Whenever you think of John or little Addie, you wonder if you could have done more.

THE END

To follow another path, turn to page 9.
To learn more about the blizzard, turn to page 103.

You're sure you recognize this haystack. You change direction and head toward home on the right path. The children are miserable and scared.

You walk and walk. The children stumble, and little Addie grows heavier with each step. Yet, you find no house and no fence. Suddenly, you think you hear a bell clanging.

"Do you hear that?" you ask.

"I do," says John. "It's straight ahead."

Someone is making that noise to guide you home. You head in that direction, praying that the angels will get you there safely.

"Let's sing my favorite hymn," you suggest. The children must keep their minds off the pain of the cold.

"Onward, Christian soldiers . . ." you begin singing. Your voice fades into the wind.

The clanging continues, and then you see a small yellow flame. Mrs. Hunt must have lit the lanterns to help you find your way.

But you're exhausted. You can't feel your legs or arms. You drop Addie into the snow and fall over her. The child isn't moving, and you can't feel her breathing. The children all huddle around you. John is the last to fall. You try to crawl along the ground, but you have no strength left. Soon the children grow silent. The last thing you remember is the sound of the clanging bell.

When they find you the next morning, you're only a short distance from the front door of the farmhouse. You have your arms wrapped around little Addie and several other children. But you've all been lost to the terrible storm.

THE END

To follow another path, turn to page 9.
To learn more about the blizzard, turn to page 103.

Search parties tied themselves together for safety as they looked for children who were missing in the storm.

CHAPTER 5
A DEADLY DAY

The Blizzard of 1888 wasn't the worst ever experienced in the Midwest, but the toll it took was terrible. Records show that between 250 and 500 people died that day, many of them children.

There were also heroes—teachers, parents, strangers, and other children—who risked their lives to bring others home to safety. Many of the stories in this book are based on real people who faced the Schoolchildren's Blizzard.

Walter Allen, the mischievous schoolboy, continued to get in trouble through his childhood. He grew up to become a reporter. He died in 1973, at the age of 93. He never forgot how his brother William had saved his life. They remained close their whole lives.

Young Lena Woebbecke fell into a coma shortly after being rescued by her Uncle Wilhelm. She eventually lost her left foot and had a wooden foot specially made for her. Her story spread far and wide by newspapers of the time.

Several brave teachers risked their own lives to help protect their students in the deadly blizzard and lead them to safety.

Teacher Etta Shattuck survived for 78 hours in a frozen haystack. She lost both legs to amputation and died of pneumonia less than a month later. A deeply religious girl, Etta told her pastor she had no regrets in life. She died two months before her 20th birthday.

Minnie Mae Freeman was another teenage teacher who saved all 16 of her students. She walked them a half mile (0.8 km) to her boarding house. Everyone survived, and Minnie Mae had a song written about her heroic efforts.

Many years after the storm, some people formed the Blizzard Club. Members gathered stories of those who had survived the storm and were still alive in 1945. Their stories were compiled into a book called *In All Its Fury*, so that people would never forget the terrible blizzard of 1888.

MORE ABOUT WINTER WEATHER

WINTER STORMS AND WEATHER FORECASTING

The science of weather forecasting was very new in the late 1800s. It was a job done by the U.S. Army Signal Corps in Washington, D.C. Smaller stations across the country sent telegraph messages to the head office several times a day. These forecasts were then printed in newspapers for everyone to read. However, not everyone would get the news in time to prepare for bad weather.

Today's world is very different from 1888. The science of meteorology has come a long way. Weather can be predicted much more accurately, and forecasts can be broadcast instantly over TV and social media. Blizzards are not uncommon, but forecasters can now warn people far in advance so they can stay safe.

FROSTBITE

Frostbite happens when your skin is exposed to extreme cold for a long time. It commonly happens to people's fingers, toes, ears, and noses. If left untreated, the skin can turn a purple-black color, and a person can lose all feeling in the area. It can also lead to dangerous infections. People with severe frostbite sometimes need to have their limbs cut off, or amputated, to save their life.

Until the 1950s, it was common for people to rub snow onto frostbitten limbs. People once believed that it was dangerous to warm up a victim too quickly. However, this was later disproven by doctors. Today, frostbite victims are warmed up quickly using warm water. You should never rub snow on the frozen areas.

HEART FAILURE

In the last story, John felt fine when he woke up after the storm but died soon after. In extreme cold, a person's body moves blood away from the skin. It goes deep into the body's core to help a person stay alive. But when a person starts moving, the blood moves quickly to the limbs and becomes chilled. When John got up and started walking, his heart would have pumped blood all over his body. But when the cold blood reached his heart, it caused an irregular heartbeat that killed him. If he had stayed in the haystack, he might have lived.

OTHER PATHS TO EXPLORE

>>> Imagine if you were a farmer living in the Midwest in 1888. You've spent several weeks huddled inside your house, worried about your sheep, goats, and cows. They need to get out into the fields to eat and move about. On January 12, the weather is so nice, you take them all out for the day. When the storm arrives suddenly, what would you do to save your animals and yourself?

>>> You wake up on January 12, 1888, and see that the weather is nice. Your family has run out of food supplies because of the long winter. You decide it would be a good day to go into town to pick up supplies. On your way back home, you encounter the terrible storm. How would you survive?

>>> If you were a child on the day of the storm, would you have gone to school? Would you bring a heavy coat, even if the weather felt warmer than usual? Think about what would've happened at school when the storm arrived. How would you have survived?

BIBLIOGRAPHY

Figley, Marty Rhodes. *The Schoolchildren's Blizzard.* Minneapolis: Lerner Books, 2004.

Laskin, David. *The Children's Blizzard.* New York: Harper Collins, 2004.

Lemke, Donald B. *The Schoolchildren's Blizzard.* North Mankato, MN: Capstone Press, 2008.

O'Gara, W. H. *In All Its Fury: A History of the Blizzard of January 12, 1888.* Lincoln, NE: Blizzard Club, 1888.

GLOSSARY

amputate (AM-pyuh-tayt)—to cut off someone's arm, leg, or other body part because it is badly damaged

divine (duh-VYNE)—something holy or sacred, relating to God

dray (DREY)—a sledge or sled, usually pulled by two horses

hymn (HIM)—a song in praise or honor of God

meteorology (mee-tee-uh-ROL-uh-jee)—the study of weather

perish (PER-ish)—to die

pneumonia (noo-MOH-nyuh)—a serious disease that causes the lungs to become swollen and filled with a thick fluid that makes breathing difficult

sepsis (SEP-suhss)—a severe, life-threatening infection of a person's blood that causes weakness, high fevers, difficulty breathing, increased heart rate, and confusion

slate (SLAYT)—a small chalk board that children once used to write on at school

smallpox (SMAWL-poks)—a disease that spreads easily from person to person and causes the skin to break out in small, pus-filled blisters that often leave deep scars

READ MORE

Drimmer, Stephanie Warren. *Ultimate Weatherpedia: The Most Complete Weather Reference Ever.* Washington, DC: National Geographic, 2019.

Tarshis, Lauren. *I Survived the Children's Blizzard, 1888.* New York: Scholastic Press, 2018.

Yomtov, Nelson. *The Children's Blizzard of 1888.* Minneapolis: Lerner Publications, 2017.

INTERNET SITES

Blizzard Brings Tragedy to Northwest Plains

history.com/this-day-in-history/blizzard-brings-tragedy-to-northwest-plains

The Schoolchildren's Blizzard of 1888

weatherology.com/trending/articles/Schoolchildrens-Blizzard.html

The Schoolchildren's Blizzard of 1888

tablerockhistoricalsociety.com/1888-schoolchildrens-blizzard.html

ABOUT THE AUTHOR

Ailynn Collins is the author of several books for kids, from stories about space and aliens, to You Choose stories and nonfiction books. She has a master's degree in writing for children and young adults from Hamline University. She's lived all over the world and speaks six languages. When she's not writing, she's competing in dog sports with one of her five dogs, or showing them in dog shows.

Photo by:
Pierre Folrev, Folrev Photography

Photo Credits
Alamy: Artokoloro, 10, ClassicStock, 88, Don Kates, 81, FLHC52, (people) Cover, History and Art Collection, 34, Nancy G Western Photography, Nancy Greifenhagen, 76, Science History Images, 86; Getty Images: Jasmin Merdan, 27, powerofforever, 107; Granger: 104, Sarin Images, 102; Newscom: Everett Collection, 6, 44; Shutterstock: Arina P Habich, 50, Barbarajo, 30, Belozorova Elena, (texture) Cover, BravissimoS, 69, KrimKate, 21, Lyubov Matveeva, 95, NatalyFox, 92, Pictureguy, 56